Little Mack's BIG Move

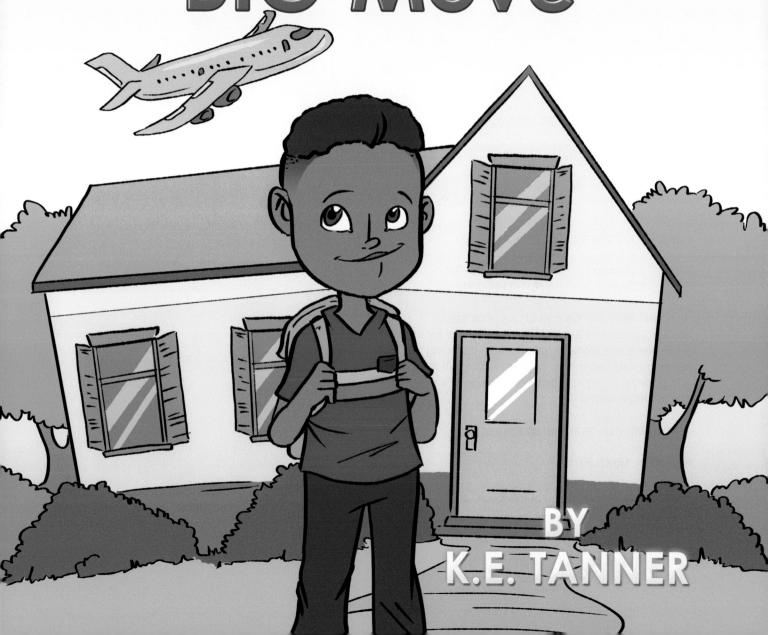

BY
K.E. TANNER

Print information available on the last page

Rev. date: 12/23/2015

To order additional copies of this book, contact:
Xlibris
1-888-795-4274
www.Xlibris.com
Orders@Xlibris.com

Little Mack's BIG Move

By
K.E. Tanner

Illustrations by
Earlene Gayle Escalona

This book is dedicated to
Dillon DeWayne Mack Adams.

Thank you for being brave
during your darkest hour.

Today was a BIG day. Today Little Mack's mom told him that they were moving to a new state.

Little Mack was very sad. He went to school and told his friends and teacher about his sad news that he and his mom were moving to new state.

Little Mack's teacher told him not to be sad. She said, "A new state means new friends and new adventures."

Little Mack loved adventures, so he thought maybe it would be fun to move to a new state.

Little Mack's teacher had Little Mack and his classmates look at maps of his new state and draw pictures of all the fun things he could do on his new adventure.

6

Little Mack and his classmates even found pictures of cacti, mountains, scorpions, and his favorite picture was a Sidewinder Rattlesnake.

Little Mack's teacher showed him pictures of the Grand Canyon and explained to him that the Grand Canyon was a great place to take adventure, since he was moving to Arizona to start a new journey.

Little Mack did not know that all of these beautiful and amazing creations were located in his new state of Arizona.

Counting down to Little Mack's moving date, his fears now turned into excitement. His teacher and friends taught him that his BIG move was a good idea and that there was nothing to fear.

Little Mack was so happy that he was able to share his feelings with his classmates, and he told them that they helped him overcome his fear.

Little Mack was now ready to take on new adventures in a new state with new friends.

The day finally came, Little Mack's BIG move. He was so excited! He waved goodbye to his teacher and to all of his friends.

13

Little Mack and his mom boarded the plane to start their journey to a new state for a new adventure. Little Mack loved planes and enjoyed their airplane ride.

A few hours passed and Little Mack officially made his BIG move. He was so excited! He saw palm trees, cacti, and bugs he had never seen before! It was amazing!

As the airplane landed, Little Mack's face was full of excitement. "This is just how I imagined it," Little Mack said to his mommy. "It is beautiful here in Arizona."

Little Mack's fears disappeared like magic! He was so happy about his BIG move.

Now he just wanted to meet some new friends and start his new adventure. Boy, was he excited!

Printed in the United States
By Bookmasters